Geese
in the
Rose Garden

By Dawn Heese

Geese in the Rose Garden

By Dawn Heese

Editor: Kimber Mitchell
Designer: Bob Deck
Photography: Aaron T. Leimkuehler
Illustration: Eric Sears
Technical Editor: Kathe Dougherty
Production assistance: Jo Ann Groves

Published by:
Kansas City Star Books
1729 Grand Blvd.
Kansas City, Missouri, USA 64108

All rights reserved
Copyright © 2009 The Kansas City Star Co.

No part of this book may be reproduced, stored in a retrieval system, or transmitted in any form or by any means, electronic, mechanical, photocopying, recording or otherwise, without the prior consent of the publisher.

First edition, first printing
ISBN: 978-1-935362-10-4

Printed in the United States of America
By Walsworth Publishing Co., Marceline, MO

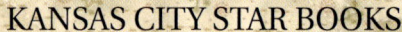
KANSAS CITY STAR BOOKS

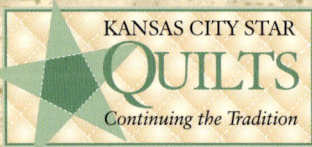

ABOUT THE AUTHOR

Dawn Heese is a third generation quilter and an avid cross stitcher. Inspired by a quilt pattern in a magazine, she bought her first rotary cutter and mat in 1999 and hasn't stopped quilting since. She particularly enjoys needleturn appliqué and hand quilting and teaches hand appliqué classes. Her love of traditional patterns stems from fond childhood memories of being surrounded by quilts.

Dawn lives in Columbia, Missouri, where she works as a hairstylist. She is a member of the Booneslick Trail Quilter's Guild as well as an appliqué group, quilt study group, and Dear Jane quilting group. Despite her busy life as mother to two teenage boys and a Great Dane, she finds time to quilt daily. *Geese in the Rose Garden* is her first book.

Table of Contents

Introduction 4
Needleturn Appliqué Instructions 6
Fabric Requirements and Supply List 8
Overdyeing Instructions 8

THE BLOCKS
Block 1: Rose Wreath 10
Block 2: Wild Goose Chase 12
Block 3: Rose of Sharon 14
Block 4: Fox and Geese 16
Block 5: Rambling Rose 18
Block 6: Brown Goose 20
Block 7: Ohio Rose 22
Block 8: Goose Tracks 24
Block 9: Rose Cross 26
Block 10: Flying Geese 28
Block 11: Rose Tree 30
Block 12: Goose in the Pond 32

FINISHING THE QUILT
Sashing 34
Borders 36

PROJECTS
Rose Parade wallhanging 41
Flying Geese pillowcase 46

Introduction

I have a passion for antiques. Whether it's vintage buttons, worn wooden washboards, or well-loved quilts, there is something special about these treasures with a sense of history. I wanted to convey that same timeworn character with my Geese in the Rose Garden quilt, while putting a fresh spin on the traditional look that its blocks are often associated with. Antique appliqué quilts often featured just a single block pattern and many—such as the red and green masterpieces of the mid to late 19th century—conveyed a decidedly formal feel. My quilt has a more casual design that mixes appliqué with pieced blocks. I also opted for a softer color palette than the typical appliqué quilts of days gone by.

The 12 blocks in Geese in the Rose Garden are all traditional in nature, some inspired by antique patterns dating back to the Civil War. Because I love the combination of appliqué and piecework, I incorporated six appliquéd rose blocks as well as six variations on geese-themed blocks. A short study of antique quilts reveals more variations of the rose block than one can imagine. There are countless versions of the Rose of Sharon block alone and the goose has lent its name to dozens of patterns as well. The appliquéd blocks in this quilt are done by hand using the needleturn method. I love the portability of hand appliqué, which allows you to take your projects wherever you go. And you can't beat the instant gratification that comes with piecing an easy quilt block. You can make endless combinations of designs with these 12 blocks—which makes this quilt an ideal choice for a block-of-the-month program.

Despite their traditional roots, the featured blocks are versatile enough to suit contemporary tastes as well. The Rose Parade wallhanging uses popular retro fabrics with a bright, modern flair. For the Geese in the Rose Garden quilt, I opted for a more muted palette of greens, reds, tans, and pinks. While they aren't reproduction fabrics, they do give the quilt a vintage feel. To soften the look, I overdyed all the pink fabric. You can use that same technique to give your quilts an instant aged appearance (To find out more about the overdyeing process, see page 8). Or, if you prefer, leave the fabrics as they are for a more updated look.

Happy quilting, *Dawn*

Dedication

To Troy, Braeden, and Eric. I love you guys so much. Thanks for understanding how someone who can manage to fit in four hours of hand quilting every day might not be able to find time to sew on a lost button.

Acknowledgements

I have so many people to thank. First and foremost, thanks to Doug Weaver and Diane McLendon of Kansas City Star Books for believing I could do this.

Thanks also to:
Kimber Mitchell, my editor, for all your work and help.

All the other dedicated people who worked on this book for turning my vision into a reality.

Bettina Havig for your unflagging patience in answering all my questions and for sharing your infinite wisdom.

Ann Rennier and Nancy Graviett for helping stitch the Rose Parade project and for always being there.

Shirley Beckett, Jane Higgins, Edie Brennan, Barb Taylor, and Lois Hassinger, you guys are the world's best support group.

Christy Gray for the beautiful quilting on Rose Parade.

Most of all, thank you to my family for being so tolerant of the many hours I spent making this book happen.

Needleturn Appliqué Instructions

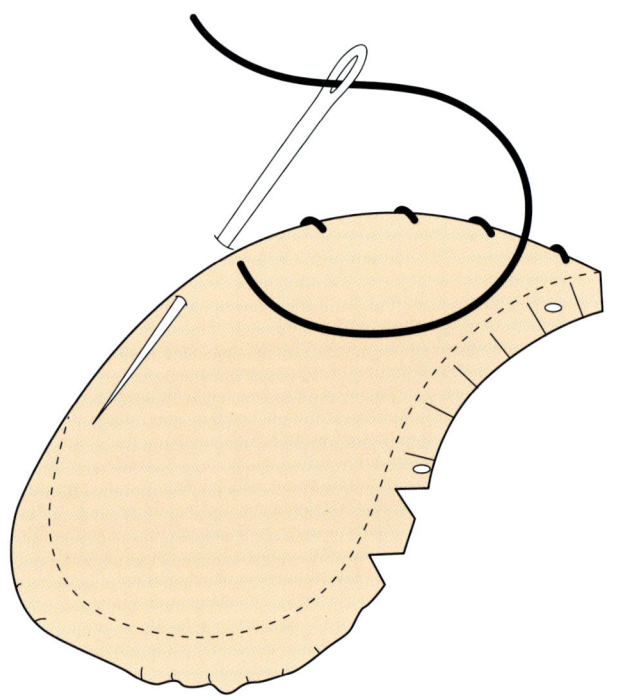

Trace template shapes to the dull side of freezer paper. Do not add seam allowances to the templates.

Iron the paper templates, shiny side down, onto the right side of fabric. Using a chalk marking pencil, trace around the template. Make sure the line is clearly visible as this will be your seam line. Add a $\frac{1}{8}$-$\frac{1}{4}$" seam allowance to the templates and cut them out.

Fold the background fabric square in half vertically and horizontally, finger pressing the fold. These fold lines will serve as a guide for placing the appliqué pieces on the fabric. Baste or pin them in place on the background square.

I recommend using YLI 100-weight silk thread in a neutral shade for your appliqué because it sinks into the fabric and practically disappears. Using a neutral color also means you won't have to worry about matching all the pieces with coordinating thread colors.

Sew the appliqué shapes in the order that they are layered, starting with the bottom pieces. Use the tip of your needle or a toothpick to turn under seam allowances.

Geese in the Rose Garden Quilt

Hand appliquéd, machine pieced, and hand quilted by Dawn Heese

Quilt size: 64" x 80½"
Finished block size: 15"

FABRIC REQUIREMENTS
- ½ yard each of two red prints
- 4 fat quarters of green prints
- 4 fat quarters of pink prints
- 3 fat quarters of brown prints
- ½ yard of dark red print for inner border
- 6 yards total of three different tan prints for background, sashing, and outer borders
- 2½ yards of 108"-wide backing fabrics
- ¾ yards of green print for binding
- Twin-sized packaged batting

GENERAL SUPPLIES
- Freezer paper
- Chalk pencil
- Silk thread, neutral color
- Bias tape makers, ¼" and ½"

OVERDYEING FABRICS

I love pink floral fabrics but they are often too bright for the palette I am working with. In fact, one of the pinks in this quilt was originally a vivid hot pink. I loved the design but the color was too loud for me. I bought it anyway and overdyed it to give it an instant aged look. Since then, I've used the fabric in several quilts. The overdyeing process I use is very simple. Fill your sink—preferably a utility sink if you have one—with very hot water. Add Rit Tan 16 liquid dye and one cup of salt (the salt helps set the dye). Add the fabric and let it soak for 20-30 minutes, stirring it occasionally. Then rinse the fabric thoroughly, toss it in the dryer, and press. If it isn't quite the color you want, simply repeat the process.

Untreated fabric   Overdyed fabric

Assembly Diagram

1. Rose Wreath
2. Wild Goose Chase
3. Rose of Sharon
4. Fox and Geese
5. Rambling Rose
6. Brown Goose
7. Ohio Rose
8. Goose Tracks
9. Rose Cross
10. Flying Geese
11. Rose Tree
12. Goose in the Pond

Geese in the Rose Garden | 9

Block 1: *Rose Wreath*

15" Finished Block

> **Tip:**
> Before starting your appliqué, it is a good idea to apply Fray Check to all the edges of the block. This will prevent it from unraveling, keeping the block true to size.

The Rose Wreath pattern has long been a popular choice for appliqué blocks. It is also referred to as Martha Washington's Wreath. Rooted in religious symbolism, the wreath itself was historically used as an embellishment for weddings and festivals. This may explain why it was often incorporated into antique wedding quilts.

HOW TO MAKE THIS BLOCK

Cut a 15½" square from one of the background fabrics. Using a ¼" bias tape maker, make a 33"-long bias stem from green fabric. With a chalk pencil, draw a circle 10" in diameter in the center of the block. This will serve as a placement guide for the wreath stem. Appliqué stem. Referring to the photo above for placement, appliqué the remaining shapes to the background fabric.

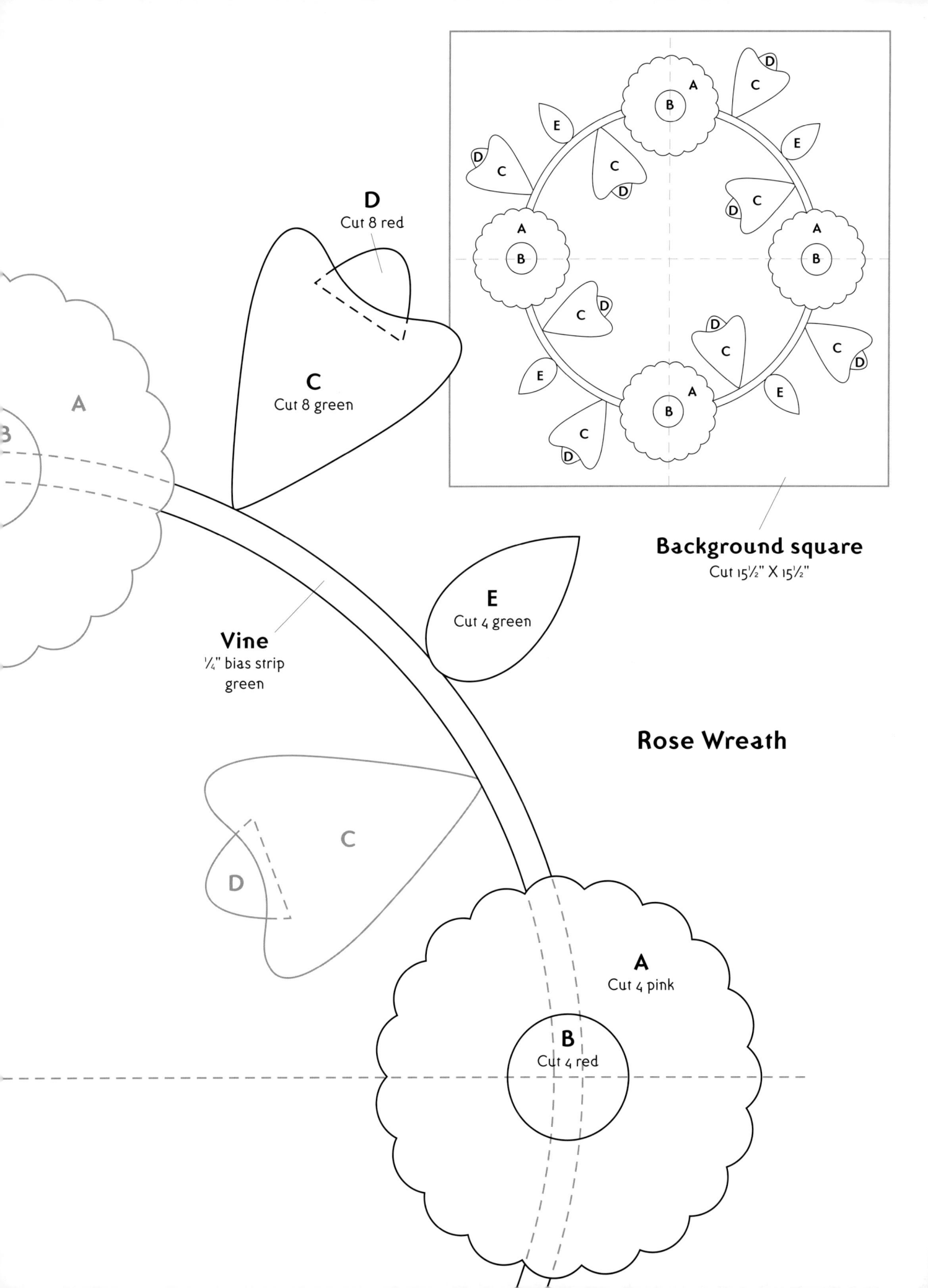

Block 2: *Wild Goose Chase*

15" Finished Block

Half-square triangles form the flying geese units in this block. By coordinating the center square fabric with the background fabric used for the four corner flying geese units, you can create an intriguing star-like design. This block isn't just great for quilts—it also makes fun table runner. For a charming table dressing, simply piece together three of the blocks and frame them with a border

CUTTING INSTRUCTIONS

All cut measurements include a ¼" seam allowance.

From background fabric, cut:

    1-11¼" square. Cut from corner to corner on the diagonal twice to yield 4 setting triangles.

From brown fabric, cut:

    1-4" square for the center.

    2-3⅜" squares. Cut from corner to corner on the diagonal once to yield 4 corner triangles.

From assorted pink/red fabrics, cut:

    16-2⅝" squares. Cut from corner to corner on the diagonal once to yield 32 half-square triangles.

From assorted green fabrics, cut:

    16-2⅝" squares. Cut from corner to corner on the diagonal once to yield 32 half-square triangles.

SEWING INSTRUCTIONS FOR WILD GOOSE CHASE

1. Pair pink/red triangles with green triangles. Then sew them right sides together to make 32 squares. Chain piecing these units will make them go faster. Trim dog ears.

2. Join two squares together to form flying geese units. Make 16 of these units.

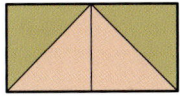

3. Join four flying geese units to make a strip. Make 4 strips.

4. Sew a brown corner triangle to the end of each flying geese strip.

5. Sew a flying geese strip to two sides of the brown center square.

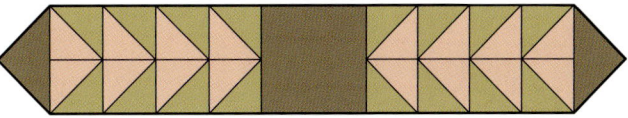

6. Sew a background setting triangle to each side of the remaining flying geese strips.

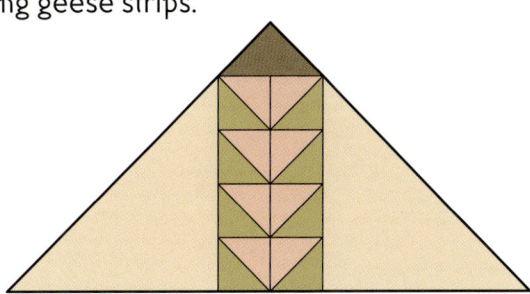

7. Join the three sections in rows to complete the block. Then press.

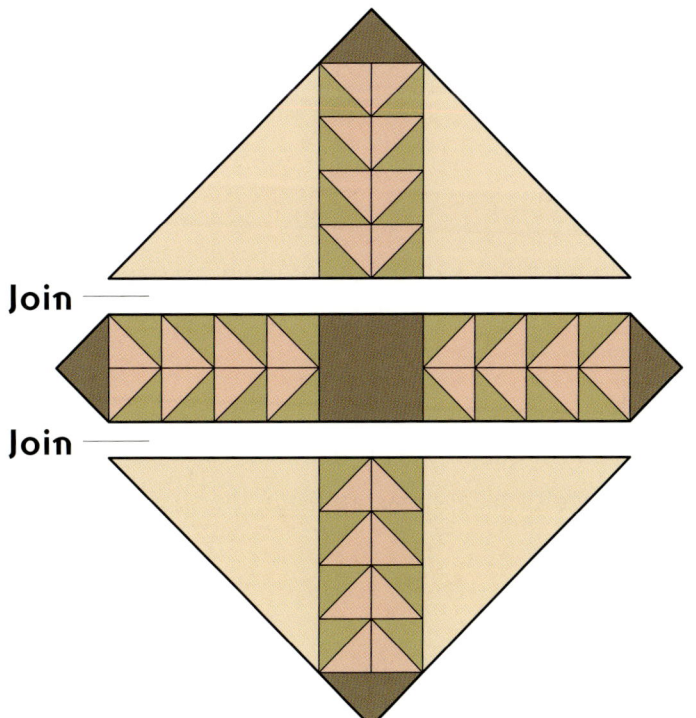

Tip: Finger pressing reduces distortion of bias pieces. Do not press with your iron until the block is complete.

Geese in the Rose Garden | 13

Block 3: *Rose of Sharon*

15" Finished Block

Numerous variations of this beloved block exist. Many of them convey a sense of formality, but this version exudes a more casual, folk art feel with its rustic star within a circle center and simple blooms.

HOW TO MAKE THIS BLOCK

From background fabric, cut one 15½" square. Using a ¼" bias tape maker, make a 48"-long bias stem from the green print. Referring to the photo above for placement, appliqué the shapes to the background fabric.

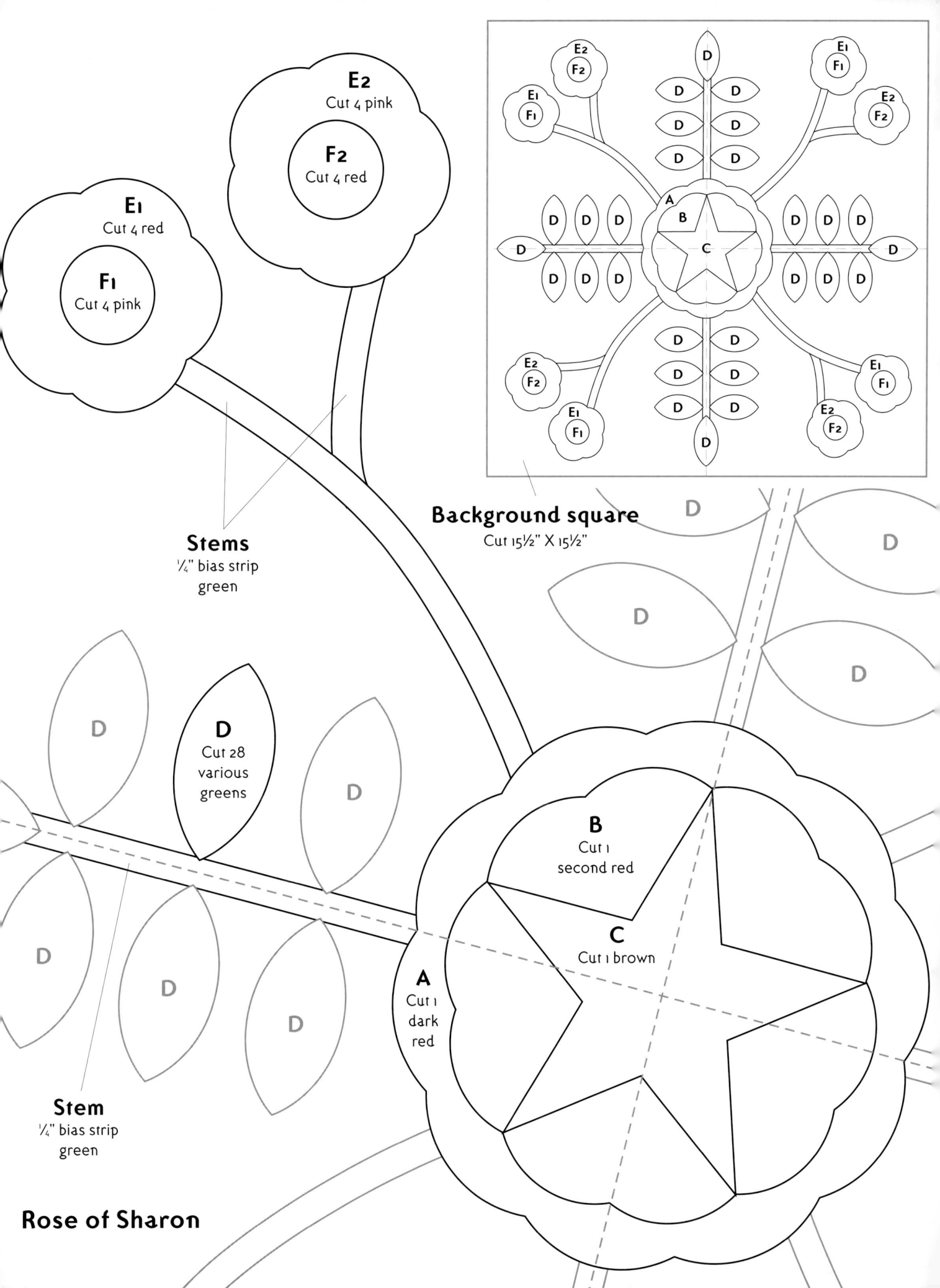

Block 4: *Fox and Geese*

15" Finished Block

This is a very simple block to piece. I used two different green prints to add visual interest. The combination of prints also gives the block a scrappier feel typical of antique quilts.

CUTTING INSTRUCTIONS

All cut measurements include a ¼" seam allowance.

From background fabric, cut:

1-8⅜" square. Cut from corner to corner on the diagonal once to yield 2 triangles.

2-4⅝" squares. Cut from corner to corner on the diagonal once to yield 4 triangles.

From assorted green fabrics, cut:

4-4¼" squares.

2-4⅝" squares. Cut from corner to corner on the diagonal once to yield 4 triangles.

1-8⅜" square. Cut from corner to corner on the diagonal once to yield 2 triangles.

SEWING INSTRUCTIONS FOR FOX AND GEESE

1. With right sides together, sew pairs of the same size background triangles to green triangles to make squares.

2. Sew one 4¼" green square to one 4¼" pieced square. Refer to diagram below for color placement.

3. Sew a second 4¼" green square to one 4¼" pieced square. Refer to diagram below for color placement.

4. Join the units to make a 4-patch block. Make 2.

5. Join one 8" pieced square to one 4-patch block. Refer to diagram below for placement. Make 2.

6. Join the 2 units to create the finished block. Then press.

Block 5: *Rambling Rose*

15" Finished Block

Rather than using the typical bud shape in my block, I opted for a layered set of circles for a more fanciful look. This block would also make a charming throw pillow for a sofa or bed. To dress it up, add buttons to the center of each circle. Or for a fun twist, make yo-yos in coordinating colors and use them in place of the buttons.

HOW TO MAKE THIS BLOCK

From background fabric, cut one 15½" square. Using a ¼" bias tape maker, make a 54"-long bias stem from green fabrics. Referring to the photo above for placement, appliqué the shapes to the background fabric.

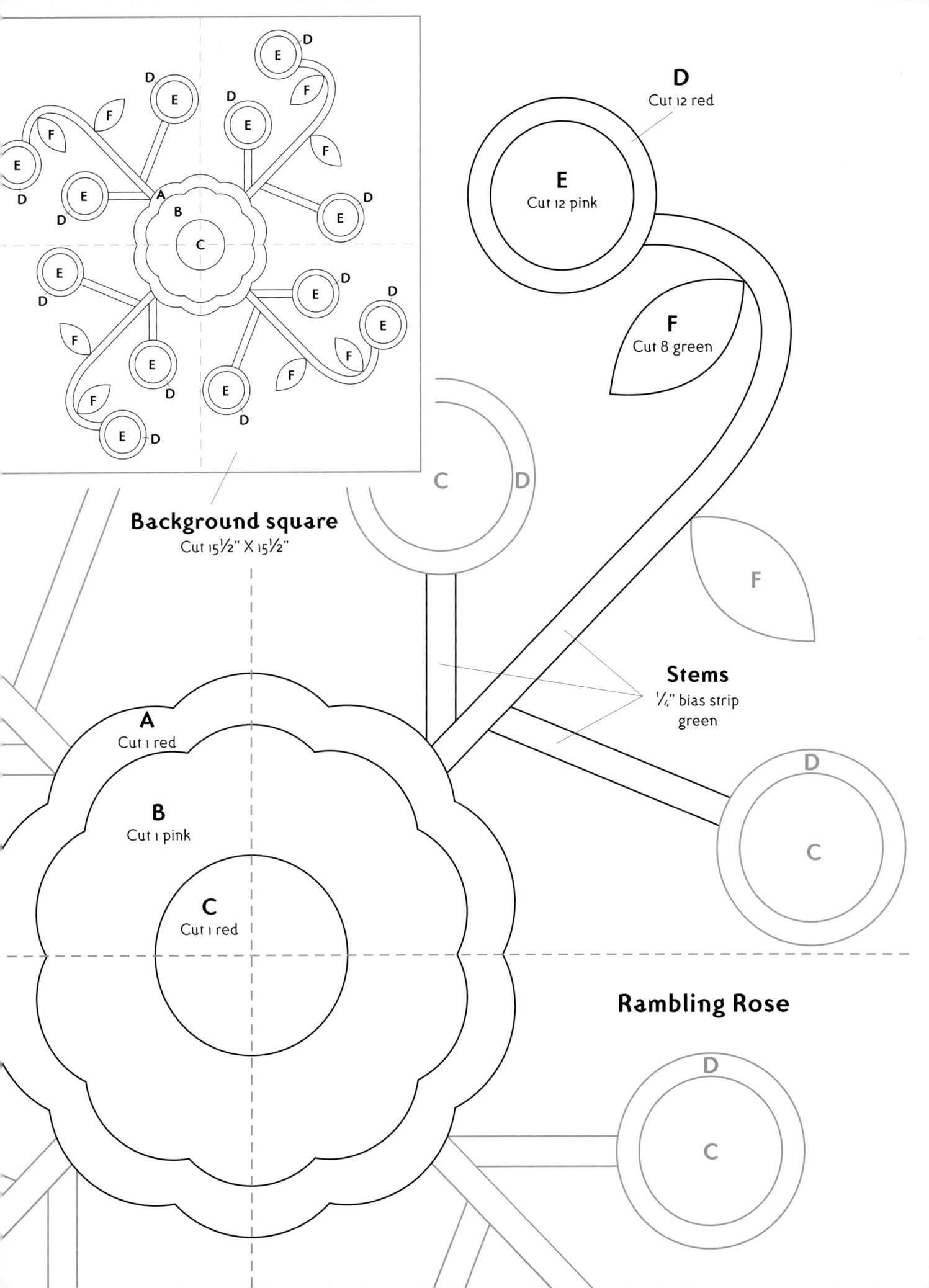

Block 6: *Brown Goose*

15" Finished Block

Historically, this block was named either Brown Goose or Gray Goose, depending on the color of the fabric. I patterned my block after the former color, but feel free to put a twist on tradition with your own favorite hue. A Blue Goose, for example, would be a fun alternative.

CUTTING INSTRUCTIONS

All cut measurements include a ¼" seam allowance.

From background fabric, cut:
 6-4⅝" squares. Cut from corner to corner on the diagonal once to yield 12 triangles.

From brown fabric, cut:
 8-4⅝" squares. Cut from corner to corner on the diagonal once to yield 16 triangles.

From pink fabric, cut:
 2-4⅝" squares. Cut from corner to corner on the diagonal once to yield 4 triangles.

SEWING INSTRUCTIONS FOR BROWN GOOSE

1. With right sides together, sew a background triangle to a brown triangle. Make 12 units.

2. With right sides together, sew a pink triangle to a brown triangle. Make 4 units.

3. Join units in rows, referring to the diagram below for color placement.

Block 7: *Ohio Rose*

15" Finished Block

You don't have to incorporate a lot of different blocks into your quilt to make a striking statement. Sometimes all you need is a single block that can stand on its own, such as this one. The Rose Parade wallhanging quilt, also featured in this book, alternates this appliquéd block with setting squares to create a fun chain effect.

HOW TO MAKE THIS BLOCK

From background fabric, cut one 15½" square. Using a ½" bias tape maker, make an 18"-long bias stem from the green print. With a chalk pencil, mark a circle 10½" in diameter in the center of the block. This will help you properly place the buds that form a circle around the center. The outer edge of the buds should align with this mark. Referring to the photo above for placement, appliqué the shapes to the background fabric.

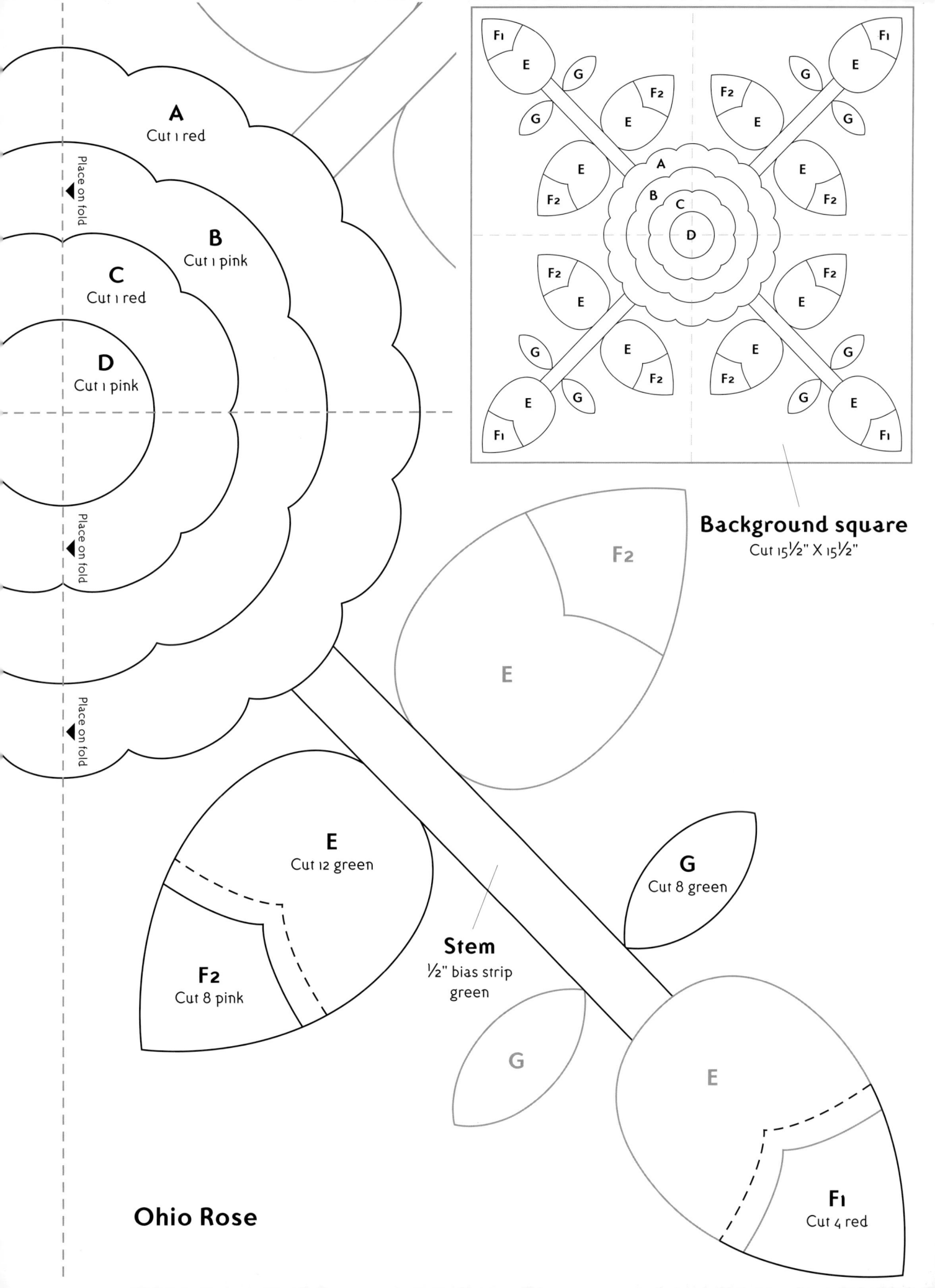

Block 8: *Goose Tracks*

15" Finished Block

I inherited a stack of Goose Track blocks made by my grandmother. While I love the blocks, I don't share her love of set-in seams. To simplify the construction of this block, I redrafted it to eliminate those intimidating set-in seams.

CUTTING INSTRUCTIONS

All cut measurements include a ¼" seam allowance.

From background fabric, cut:

    4-2½" squares.

    8-2⅞" squares. Cut from corner to corner on the diagonal once to yield 16 triangles.

    4-3½" x 6½" rectangles.

From brown fabric, cut:

    4-2½" squares.

    1-3½" square.

    4-2⅞" squares. Cut from corner to corner on the diagonal once to yield 8 triangles.

From pink fabric, cut:
  8-2⅞" squares. Cut from corner to corner on the diagonal once to yield 16 triangles.

From red fabric, cut:
  8-2⅞" squares. Cut from corner to corner on the diagonal once to yield 16 triangles.

SEWING INSTRUCTIONS FOR GOOSE TRACKS

1. With right sides together, sew:
   - A pink triangle to a background triangle. Make 8 units.
   - A red triangle to a background triangle. Make 8 units.
   - A red triangle to a pink triangle. Make 4 units.
   - A red triangle to a brown triangle. Make 4 units.
   - A pink triangle to a brown triangle. Make 4 units.

2. Referring to the diagram below for color placement, sew units in rows to create a Goose Track unit. To reduce bulk, press the seams open. Make 4 units.

3. Join 2 Goose Track units with a 3½" x 6½" rectangle to make the top section of the block. Repeat this step for the bottom section.

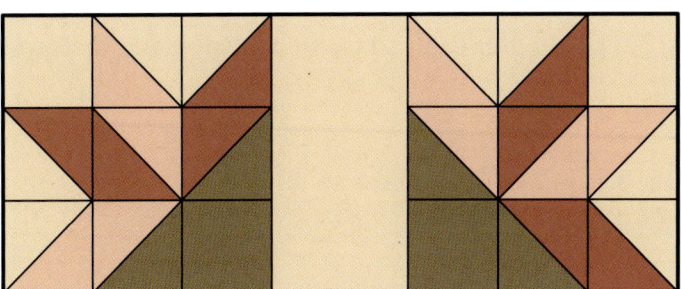

4. Attach 2-3½" x 6½" rectangles to opposite sides of the brown 3½" square to make the center row of the block.

5. Join the three rows to complete the block. Press.

Geese in the Rose Garden | 25

Block 9: *Rose Cross*

15" Finished Block

I love the geometric look of the kite-shaped leaves in this block. I swapped the placement of the light and dark green leaves by accident, creating a more informal design. But I liked the result so much that I decided to keep it.

HOW TO MAKE THIS BLOCK

From the background fabric, cut one 15½" square. Using a ½" bias tape maker, make an 18"-long bias stem from the green print. Referring to the photo above for placement, appliqué shapes to the background fabric.

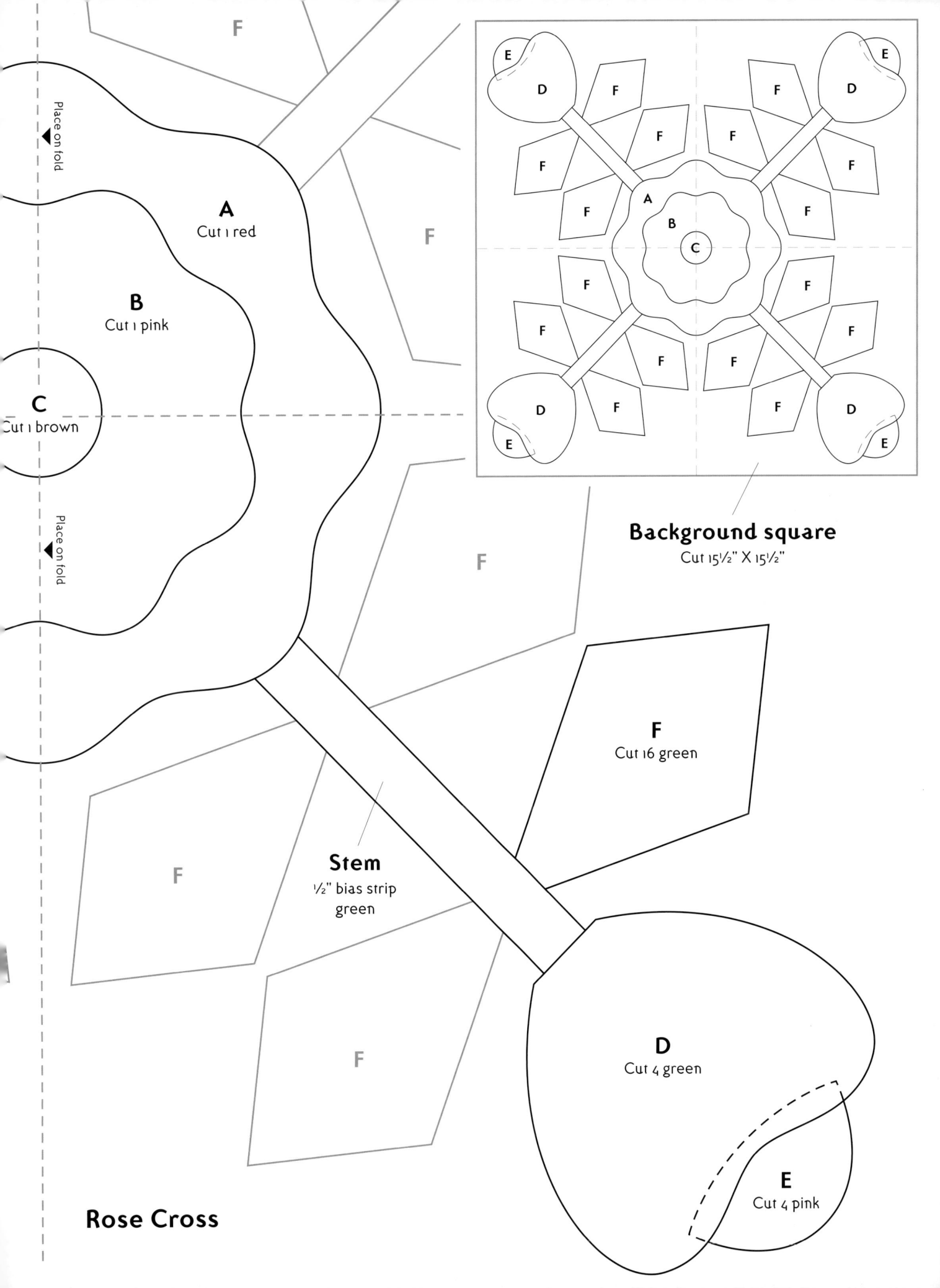

Block 10: *Flying Geese*

15" Finished Block

Traditional flying geese units require precise piecing skill to create sharp points, but this block makes it easy to achieve them. That's because the measurements for the flying geese units build in more room between the tip of the points and the next flying geese unit. The result is a picture-perfect finish without the worry of cutting off points.

CUTTING INSTRUCTIONS

All cut measurements include a ¼" seam allowance.

From assorted brown fabrics, cut:
15 - 3½" x 5½" rectangles.

From assorted pink fabrics, cut:
30 - 3½" squares.

SEWING INSTRUCTIONS FOR FLYING GEESE

1. With right sides together, lay a pink square on one corner of a brown rectangle. Sew from corner to corner on the diagonal.

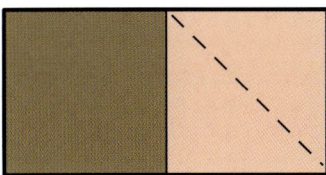

2. Cut the corner, leaving a ¼" seam allowance. Then press the triangle open.

3. Repeat on the other side of the rectangle to make a flying geese unit. Make 15 units.

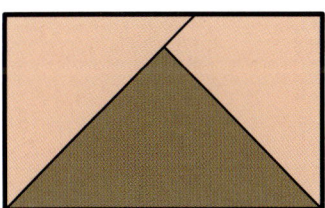

4. Join 5 flying geese units to make a vertical row. Make 3 units.

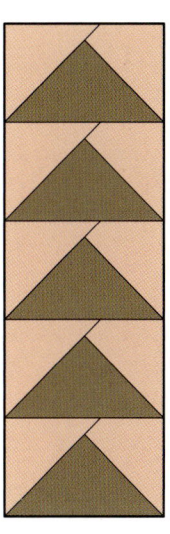

5. Join the three rows to complete the block. Press.

Block 11: *Rose Tree*

15" Finished Block

This block looks great in a traditional color palette of red and green against a muslin background. You could easily adapt it into a wallhanging by enlarging the templates to create 18" blocks. Simply combine four of the 18" blocks, add a border, and you have a wonderful heirloom quilt that's sure to warm up a bland wall.

HOW TO MAKE THIS BLOCK

From the background fabric, cut one 15½" block. Using a ½" bias tape maker, make a 25"-long bias stem from green print. Referring to the photo above for placement, appliqué shapes to the background fabric.

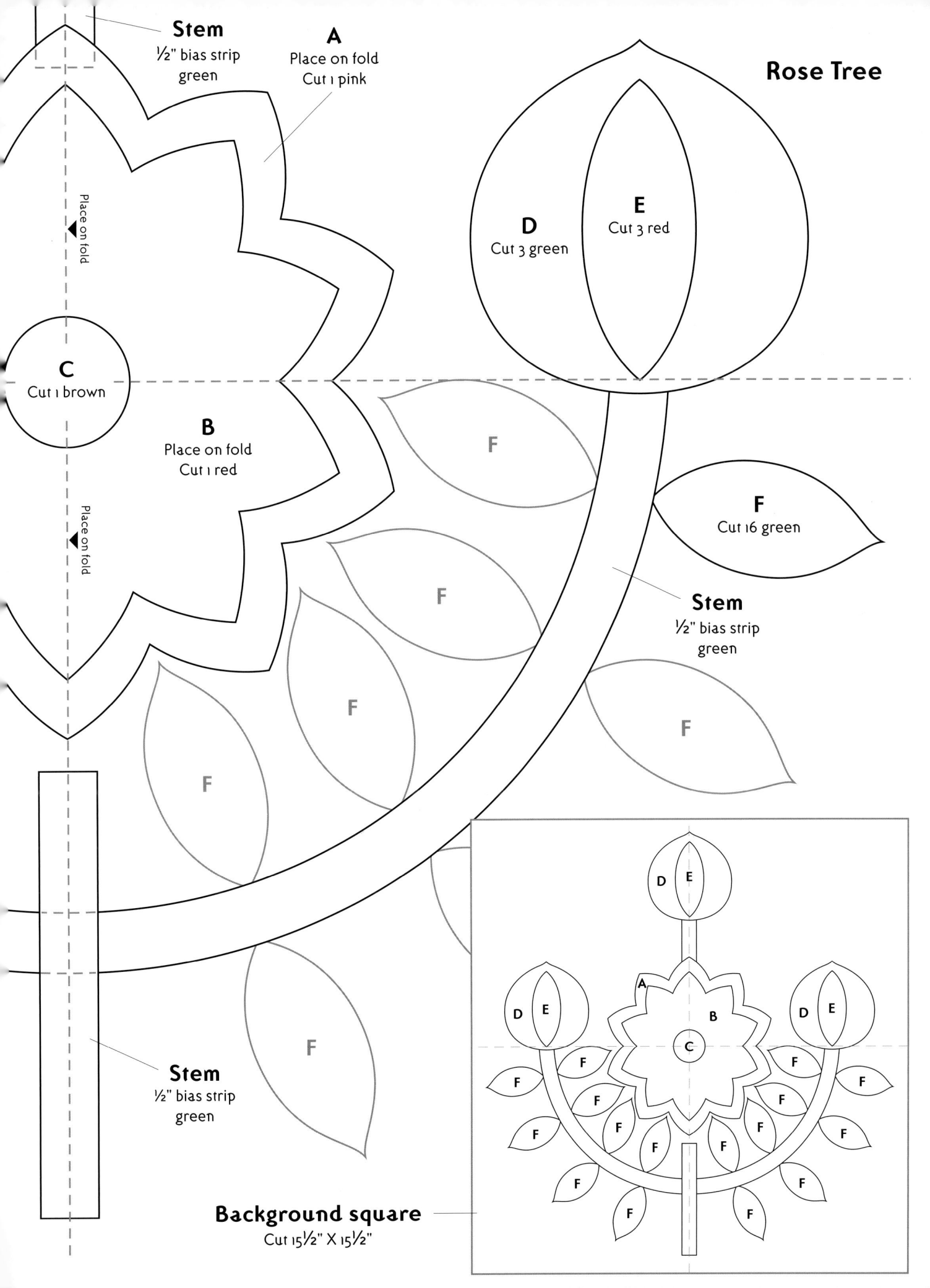

Block 12: *Goose in the Pond*

15" Finished Block

Like many quilt patterns of the past, this one is known by multiple names, including Missouri Puzzle. A quilt made entirely of this block makes a stunning centerpiece for any room. When combined, the blocks form a secondary pattern that adds intrigue to the overall composition.

CUTTING INSTRUCTIONS

All cut measurements include a ¼" seam allowance.

From background fabric, cut:

6–3⅞" squares. Cut from corner to corner on the diagonal once to yield 12 triangles.
5–3½" squares.
2–1½" x 13" strips.
1–1½" x 14" strip.
1–1½" x 7" strip.

From green fabric, cut:

6–3⅞" squares. Cut from corner to corner on the diagonal once to yield 12 triangles.

From red fabric, cut:
- 1–1½" x 13" strip.
- 2–1½" x 14" strips.
- 2–1½" x 7" strips.

SEWING INSTRUCTIONS FOR GOOSE IN THE POND

1. With right sides together, sew a green triangle to a background triangle. Make 12 units.

2. Sew a 1½" x 14" red strip to each side of a 1½" x 14" background strip. Press. Cut into 3½" units. Make 4 units.

3. Sew a 1½" x 7" red strip to each side of a 1½" x 7" background strip. Press. Cut into 1½" units. Make 4 units.

4. Sew a 1½" x 13" background strip to each side of a 1½" x 13" red strip. Press. Cut into 1½" units. Make 8 units.

5. Sew units together to make 9-patch units. Make four of these units. See the figure below for color placement.

6. Referring to figure below, sew units into rows. Then join rows to complete the block. Press.

Geese in the Rose Garden | 33

Finishing the Quilt: Sashing

Now that you have made your blocks, it is time to finish the quilt. Before deciding on a final placement for all my blocks, I experimented with a variety of options until I liked the arrangement. You can follow my layout or mix it up for your own unique version.

CUTTING INSTRUCTIONS
All cut measurements include a ¼" seam allowance.

From background fabrics, cut:
  17-2" x 15½" strips.
From red fabric, cut:
  3-2" squares.
  24-1¼" squares.
From pink fabric, cut:
  3-2" squares.
  24-1¼" squares.

SEWING INSTRUCTIONS

1. With right sides together, lay a 1¼" red square on one end of a sashing strip. Sew from corner to corner on the diagonal. Cut the corner, leaving a ¼" seam allowance. Then press in place.

2. Repeat the above step with another 1¼" red square on the other corner of the same end of the sashing strip. Then press in place. These sashing units will create the star points.

3. Sew this sashing strip between Block 1 and Block 2. The points should be at the bottom of the blocks. Make another sashing strip with the pink points on one end only. Sew this strip between Block 2 and Block 3. The points should be at the bottom of the blocks.

4. Make 4 sashing strips with red points on one end and pink points on the other end. Then sew:
- A strip between Block 4 and Block 5. The red points should be at the top of the blocks.
- A strip between Block 5 and Block 6. The red points should be at the bottom of the blocks.
- A strip between Block 7 and Block 8. The red points should be at the bottom of the blocks.
- A strip between Block 8 and Block 9. The red points should be at the top of the blocks.

5. Make a sashing strip with red points on one end only.

6. Make a sashing strip with pink points on one end only.

7. Sew the sashing strip with red points between Block 10 and Block 11. The points should be at the top of the blocks.

8. Sew the sashing strip with pink points between Block 11 and Block 12. The points should be at the top of the blocks.

JOINING THE ROWS

1. Make a sashing strip with red points on one end. Join the pointed end to a 2" red square.

2. Make a sashing strip with red points on one end and pink points on the other end. Join the red end to the opposite side of the 2" red square from the above step.

3. Join a 2" pink square to the pink pointed end of the strip.

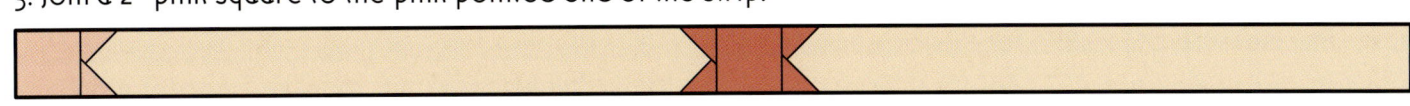

4. Make a sashing strip with pink points and sew it to the opposite side of the 2" pink square. This will be the sashing that connects the rows. Make 3 of these strips.

5. Referring to the diagram below, join the rows with the sashing strips.

Geese in the Rose Garden | 35

Finishing the Quilt: Adding the Borders

Quantities are based on 44" width fabric.
All cut measurements include a ¼" seam allowance.

INNER BORDER

From dark red fabric, cut six strips 2½" x the width of the fabric. Cut and piece these strips to make 2 border strips that measure 2½" x 48½" for the top and bottom and 2 strips that measure 2½" x 69" for the sides. Sew the top and bottom strips first, then the side strips.

OUTER BORDER

Each side of the outer border is constructed differently, so separate instructions are listed for each. The outer border consists of three different background fabrics, which are labeled #1, #2, and #3 in the instructions.

TOP OUTER BORDER

From background fabric #3, cut 1-6½" x 26¼" strip. From background fabric #2, cut 1-6½" x 27¼" strip. Join the two strips to make the top border. Sew the border strip to the top of the quilt center. Background fabric #2 should be on the right.

BOTTOM OUTER BORDER

Cutting Instructions for Flying Geese Units:
From assorted prints, cut 22-3½" x 6½" rectangles.
From background fabric #1, cut 44-3½" squares.

1. With right sides together, lay a background square on a rectangle. Sew from corner to corner on the diagonal. Cut the corner, leaving a ¼" seam allowance. Press open.

2. Repeat on the other end to make a flying geese unit. Make 22 units.

3. Join 11 flying geese units to make a border strip. Make 2 strips.

4. From background fabric #2, cut one 6½" x 19½" strip. Join the strip to one of the flying geese strips. The points should go toward the background strip.

5. Referring to the quilt diagram on the next page, sew the border strip to the bottom of the quilt center. The flying geese units should be on the right side.

LEFT OUTER BORDER

1. From background fabric #2, cut 1-6½" x 41¾" strip.

2. From background fabric #3, cut 1-6½" x 40¼" strip. Join the two strips to make the left border. Sew the border strip to the left side of the quilt. Background fabric #3 should be at the top of the quilt.

RIGHT OUTER BORDER

1. From background fabric #2, cut 1-6½" x 42" strip.

2. From background fabric #1, cut 1-6½" square. Join the flying geese strip to the 6½" square. The flying geese should be pointing away from the square.

3. Sew the 6½" x 42" strip to the other end of the flying geese strip. Sew this border to the right side of the quilt. The 6½" square should be at the bottom.

Geese in the Rose Garden | 37

Finishing the Quilt: Border Appliqué

The appliquéd portion of the border is the result of experimenting with different placements for the flowers and leaves. To begin, I laid out all the appliqué pieces on the top and left border strips. Then I moved them around until I found an arrangement that was pleasing to the eye. All of the appliqué templates for the border are from the blocks featured in the quilt.

From Rose Wreath (Block 1):
    C-Cut 4 green
    D-Cut 4 red

From Rose of Sharon (Block 3):
    C-Cut 2 red

From Rambling Rose (Block 5):
    D-Cut 4 red
    E-Cut 4 pink

From Ohio Rose (Block 7):
    F2-Cut 2 pink
    E-Cut 2 green

From Rose Cross (Block 9):
    A-Cut 1 red
    B-Cut 1 pink
    C-Cut 1 brown
    D-Cut 2 green
    E-Cut 2 pink
    F-Cut 4 green

From Rose Tree (Block 11):
    F-Cut 4 green
    E-Cut 6 green

CUTTING INSTRUCTIONS

For the stems:
    Using a ½" bias tape maker, make two 39"-long stems.
    Using a ¼" bias tape maker, make a 12"-long stem.
        Cut the stem to yield two 3½"-long stems.
    Cut the remaining part to yield two 2½"-long stems.

For approximate placement of appliqué, refer to the diagram on page 39.

Once the entire quilt top has been assembled, quilt as desired and bind. For binding, I used a dark green print.

Border Appliqué Guide Diagram

Geese in the Rose Garden | 39

Projects

40 | Geese in the Rose Garden

Rose Parade Wallhanging Quilt

Quilt size: 56" x 56"
Finished block size: 14"

*Machine pieced and hand appliquéd by Dawn Heese
Machine quilted by Christy Gray/Katydid Design Studio*

Rose Parade is designed to showcase a more modern spin on one of the blocks used in the feature quilt. I am intrigued by all the retro fabrics on the market today and wanted to find a way to incorporate them into my quilts, but I knew making a quilt entirely of these fabrics would push me too far out of my comfort zone. So I decided to use them just for my appliqué while relying on the more traditional fabrics for the block backgrounds and outer borders. The result is the perfect fusion of new and old. The retro fabrics make the appliqué pop and the classic background fabrics soften the overall effect, keeping the showier retro fabrics from overpowering the quilt. The lesson is: If you see a fabric you like but don't think it fits your style, buy it anyway. You might be surprised by how well it goes with your typical fabric choices!

This quilt also demonstrates how you can use a single block pattern to create a whole new quilt. The templates for this appliqué block are the same ones used in the Ohio Rose block (Block 7) of the Geese in the Rose Garden quilt. The only change is the size of the background squares. Instead of a 15" finished block, you will have a 14" finished block. As a result, the appliqué shapes will fit a little closer together. You can easily turn Rose Parade into a bed quilt by adding more blocks. A 4 x 5 block setting will create a twin-size quilt.

Rose Parade Wallhanging Quilt

FABRIC REQUIREMENTS

- ⅞ yard each of three different background fabrics (The cross-stitch patterned background fabric is Blackbird Designs at Water's Edge by Moda)
- ½ yard of retro green print for stems and bud cups
- ½ yard of light red paisley print for corner buds and largest rose
- ¼ yard of dotted red print for second largest rose
- Fat quarter of green and white print for leaves
- Fat quarter of pink print with large dot for buds
- Fat quarter of pink print with small dot for smallest rose
- Scraps of dotted yellow print for center circles
- ¾ yard of pink print with large dot for inner border and binding
- 1¼ yards of small cream print for outer border
- 65" square of batting
- 4 yards backing fabric

CUTTING INSTRUCTIONS

All cut measurements include a ¼" seam allowance.

From background fabrics, cut:
    9-14½" squares.

From pink with large dot fabric, cut:
    5-1½" strips the width of fabric.

From small cream print, cut:
    6-6½" strips the width of fabric.

SEWING INSTRUCTIONS

1. Make 5 Ohio Rose appliquéd blocks. Referring to the diagram below for placement, sew appliquéd blocks to setting squares to form rows. Then join rows to make the quilt center.

2. Join the dotted pink 1½" strips to make 2-1½" x 42" strips. Sew to the top and bottom of the quilt center. Join the remaining dotted pink 1½" strips to make 2-1½" x 44½" strips. Sew to the sides of the quilt center.

3. Join the small cream print 6½" strips to make 2-6½" x 44½" strips. Sew to the top and bottom of the quilt center.

4. Join the remaining small cream print 6½" strips to make 2-6½" x 56½" strips. Sew to both sides of the quilt.

WORKING WITH SCALLOPS

1. The quilt should be quilted BEFORE you make your scallops. Then trace the scallop templates on pages 44 and 45 to freezer paper and cut along the traced line.

2. Using a chalk pencil, mark the scallops on all sides of the front of the quilt. Do NOT cut on the marked line because it will be the sewing line.

3. Using the pink print with large dot, make bias binding. Since the border of this quilt is scalloped, you must use bias strips for the binding. These have a natural stretch to them that allows you to easily follow the curves of the quilt.

4. Starting on the rounded part of the scallop, sew the binding on the marked line, using a ¼" seam allowance and aligning the raw edges of the binding with the marked line. Stitch to the base of the valley between the scallops. Stop with the needle down, pivot, then sew out of the valley. Be careful to avoid creating pleats. Once the binding has been sewn in place, cut away the excess border. Turn the binding over to the back of the quilt and hand stitch it in place.

Reverse this corner template for opposite corners

Corner

**Scallop Border
Template - part 1**

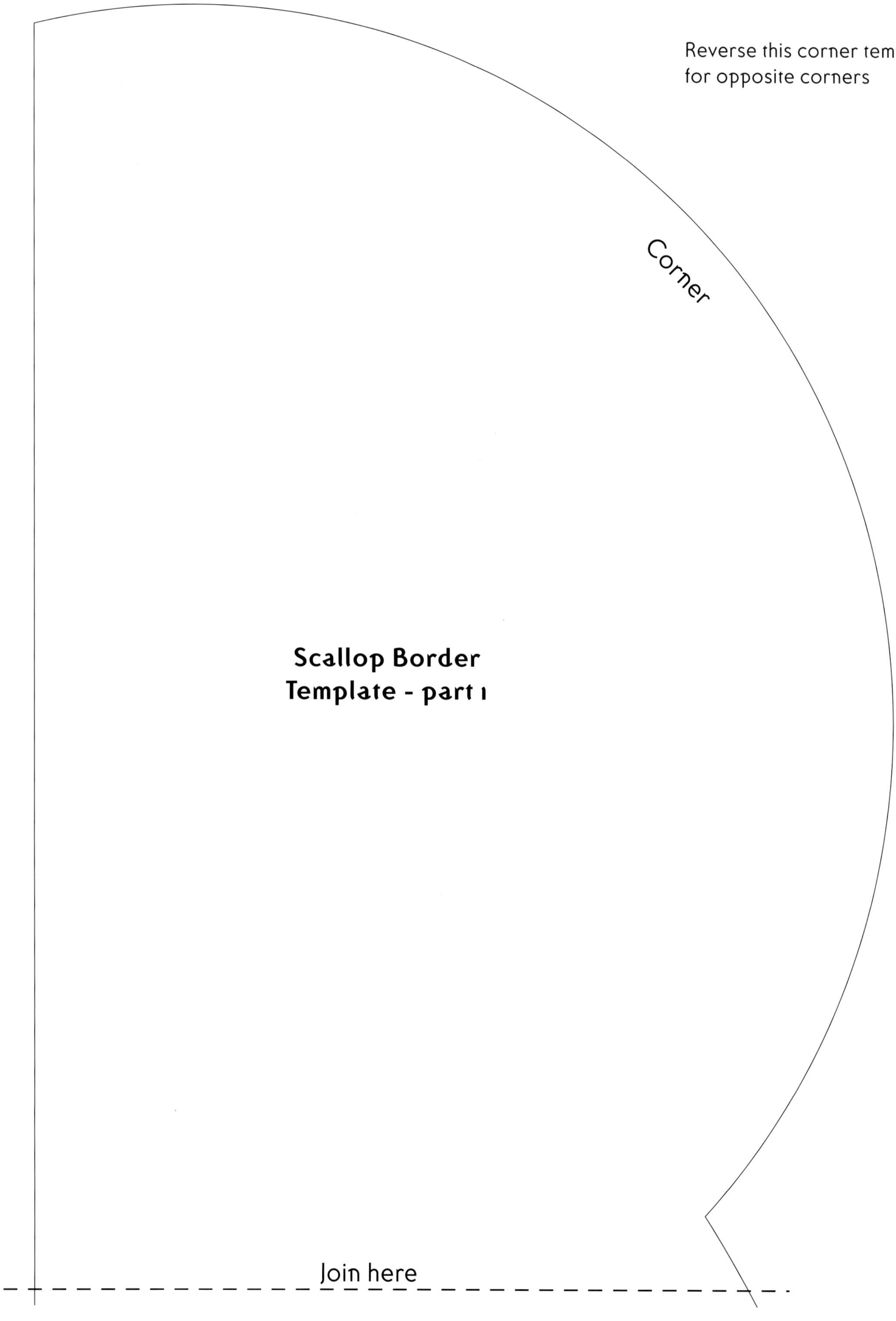

Join here

Join here

**Scallop Border
Template - part 2**

Flying Geese Pillowcase

Machine pieced by Dawn Heese

Making your own pillowcases to match a quilt is a fast and easy way to dress up a bed. This flying geese pillowcase is simple to stitch, and it makes a fun gift. After all, who can resist a cozy handmade pillowcase? Stitch up a pair of them, tie them with ribbon, and give them to a friend.

FABRIC REQUIREMENTS

These measurements will make one pillowcase.
- 1 yard of brown fabric for the pillowcase body and flying geese background
- ⅛ yard of dark red fabric for accent strip
- ¼ yard of pink fabric for inner lining
- Scraps, at least 4" x 7" for each of 14 flying geese units

CUTTING INSTRUCTIONS

All cut measurements include a ¼" seam allowance.

From brown fabric, cut:
    1-26" x 42½" piece.
    28-3½" squares.

From red fabric, cut:
    1-1" x 42½" strip.

From pink fabric, cut:
    1-7½" x 42½" strip.

From scraps, cut:
    14-3½" x 6½" rectangles.

SEWING INSTRUCTIONS

1. With right sides together, lay one brown 3½" square on one end of a 3½" x 6½" rectangle. Sew from corner to corner on the diagonal. Cut the corner, leaving a ¼" seam allowance. Then press.

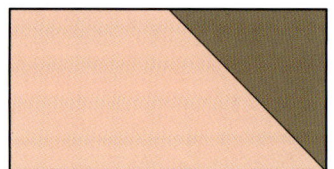

2. Repeat on the other end to make a flying geese unit. Make 14.

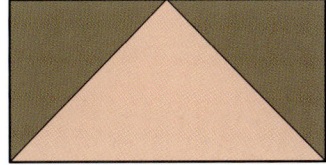

3. With right sides together, sew the 1" x 42½" red strip to the brown pillowcase body. Press the seam toward the red strip.

4. Join the flying geese units to make a strip that measures 6½" x 42½". With right sides together, sew this strip to the red strip of the pillowcase unit.

5. With right sides together, sew the pink 7½" strip to the flying geese strip in the pillowcase body.

6. Press under ½" along the raw edge of the pink strip. With right sides together, fold the pillowcase in half horizontally and sew the bottom and side closed.

7. Keeping the pillow wrong side out, fold the pink strip to the inside, aligning the pressed edge with the line of stitching between the main body and the red strip. Blind stitch the pressed edge to the seam allowance so it doesn't show through to the right side. Turn the finished pillowcase right side out and press.

Geese in the Rose Garden | 47

Quick and Easy Pincushion

When auditioning different flying geese units for my quilt and pillowcase, I ended up with several that didn't make it into the finished projects. A great way to use up those leftovers is to turn them into pincushions. They make handy accessories for your sewing area as well as practical yet pretty gifts for your quilting friends. Simply choose a 3½" x 6½" piece of fabric in a coordinating print for the pincushion backing. With right sides together, sew the backing to the flying geese unit, using a ¼" seam allowance and leaving a 1-inch-wide opening for stuffing. Turn right side out. Fill the pincushion with fiberfill or sand. Then slipstitch the opening closed.